ADVENT CONSPIRACY

ADVENT CONSPIRACY

CAN CHRISTMAS STILL CHANGE THE WORLD?

RICK MCKINLEY, CHRIS SEAY, AND GREG HOLDER

ZONDERVAN®

ZONDERVAN.com/
AUTHORTRACKER
follow your favorite authors

ZONDERVAN

Advent Conspiracy

This title is also available as a Zondervan ebook.
Visit www.zondervan.com/ebooks.

This title is also available in a Zondervan audio edition.
Visit www.zondervan.fm.

Requests for information should be addressed to:

Zondervan, *Grand Rapids, Michigan 49530*

Library of Congress Cataloging-in-Publication Data

McKinley, Rick.
Advent conspiracy : can Christmas still change the world? / Rick McKinley, Chris Seay, and Greg Holder ; with contributions from co-conspirators around the world.
p. cm.
Includes bibliographical references.
ISBN 978-0-310-32452-2 (softcover)
1. Christmas. 2. Consumption (Economics)—Religious aspects—Christianity. I. Seay, Chris. II. Holder, Greg, 1961- III. Title.
BV45.M43 2009
263'.915—dc22 2009023110

Published in association with Yates & Yates, www.yates2.com.

Interior design: Beth Shagene

Printed in the United States of America

13 14 15 16 17 /DCI/ 25 24 23 22 21 20 19 18 17 16 15 14 13 12

CONTENTS

[1]

A PROPHETIC DREAM

Imagine: The Creator of the cosmos chose, from among his numberless galaxies and spinning stars, one tiny rock of a planet on which to enter human life in the most natural and self-effacing of ways—through the womb of an unwed teenage girl.

His was one of many births that night, no doubt, but it was unique: God became a wailing, wrinkled newborn birthed onto the bloody straw of life on our sin-sick planet.

Perhaps only the angels knew what they were really witnessing. Their voices rang through the heavens, singing, "Glory to God in the highest!" Glory to God for the gift of his son; glory to God for the cosmos-dwarfing love that led to the birth of a King in a rough stable.

There is a sense of prophetic mystery surrounding Christ's birth. The story reveals something divine to us; it drives our quest to look closely at our own stories. *Who are we? Why are we? How do we? Where, in the midst of our questions, is this Immanuel, this God-with-us?*

MISSING OUT

Sadly, for all our questioning, the mystery of the Incarnation escapes us. Jesus comes, in his first Advent, into the midst of our great sin and suffering. This was God's design. But apart from the angels nudging a few scared shepherds and a cryptic star decoded by a handful of distant astrologists, almost everyone else missed it.

Missing out should feel familiar; most of us habitually miss it every year at Christmas. Our story is consumption and consumerism, and we're obsessed with the climax. We worship less. We spend more. We give less. We struggle more.

Less, more. More, less. Time and nerves stretch thin, and we reduce family and friends to a card or a present that costs the "right" amount to prove our level of love. Our quest to celebrate mystery exhausts us. Another Christmas passes by like a blizzard, and we are left to shovel through the trash of our failure.

Missing the prophetic mystery of Jesus' birth means missing God-with-us, God beside us — God becoming one of us. Missing out on Jesus changes everything.

BACK TO THE STABLE

Several years ago a few of us friends were lamenting how much we hate pastoring at Christmas. We shared our dread of preparing to proclaim, celebrate, and worship Jesus at his Incarnation while we — along with our congregations — are consumed with idolatry.

We become lost in crowded malls, financial debt, and endless lists of gifts to buy. The false doctrine of consumer religion insists, again and again, that money equals love — a convincing enough tale to make believers out of non-Christians and Christians alike.

We were afraid that on Christmas day, God would come near — as he always does and always is — and we would miss it yet again.

So we decided to try an experiment: What if, instead of acting like bystanders to the nativity, we led our congregations *into* the nativity story as participants?

We didn't know what to expect, but we knew we needed to reclaim the story of Christmas, the foundational narrative of the church. As we strove to see the birth of Christ from inside the stable instead of inside the mall, our holiday practices began to change.

SPEND LESS.
GIVE MORE.
WORSHIP FULLY.

If it doesn't take money to love, a recalculation is needed. If love is to be the driving force of our gift-giving, then money cannot be. Our dominating culture of consumerism can, and must, be rejected. When we refuse to equate money with love, we become free. Free to leave the shallow story of cultural Christmas and enter the deep, life-giving waters of the Incarnation. Free to give without comparison, receive with gratitude, and worship with abandon.

Children understand the creative joy of making gifts,

the excitement of giving themselves away. Watching our own children, and receiving their love, we remembered that we didn't need a price tag to quantify our love. Spending less freed us to give more. We replaced material presents with the gift of presence. We learned to give our time, our talents, our love, and ourselves to one another.

We were convinced that an inescapable consequence of truly entering the Christmas story was compulsion to love all. We were reminded of Jesus' teaching that, whenever we see a brother or sister hungry or cold, whatever we do to the least of these, so we do to him. To love Jesus, we needed to love and serve the outcast, poor, and ignored among us — in our local schools, in Liberian villages, and under highway overpasses as the mechanisms of progress sped by.

Spending less gave us the resources to make a huge difference — and the greatest resource was the presence of Christ within us. With our new freedom of time-space and mind-space, our attention was more fully focused on Jesus' coming. For the first time in many years, we felt as if we were on our knees in the dirt beside the manger, worshiping with the shepherds. Jesus was being experienced among us in living, transforming, beautiful, and fresh ways, and the stories of changed lives multiplied greater than we could ever imagine. Nothing seemed impossible for God . . . and it didn't stop at Christmas.

DREAMING BIGGER DREAMS

When we considered that the coming of Christ was good news for all people, we began to realize that meant everyone. Not just our friends and neighbors but *everyone*. All people for all time. So we began to think of how this announcement could show up in tangible ways all over the world. One of our friends began to be burdened about the world water crisis.

The water crisis around the world is staggering. Hundreds of children die simply because they don't have access to clean drinking water. It makes our mouths drop and our stomachs turn when we realize that the amount of money we spend on Christmas in America is close to forty-five times the amount of money it would take to supply the entire world with clean water. What if some of the money we spent at Christmas was used to dig wells for poor or remote communities in which people die regularly from the lack of clean water? So, partnering with Living Water International, we used the money we saved from worshiping more and spending less to build many wells.

We will never forget receiving the email telling us that the water crisis in Mount Barclay, Liberia, was solved! Children splashing the fresh water and praising God simply because people on the other side of the world began to be more faithful to the message of Christmas.

Over the last few years, we traveled at Christmas to these villages with new wells to celebrate the hope of Jesus with them. Imagine children dancing and shouting as clean water gushes into the air. Picture people worshiping Jesus with cup after cup: "Living water for our souls, clean water for our bodies." Consider that each well was drilled with money that was rightly given as a birthday gift to our liberating King.

It wasn't just wells either; there were tangible local expressions that the announcement of Christ was good news to the least of these in our own communities. One church threw open the doors at the local school so 150 of the poorest families in their community could come and receive clothing, food, and some simple gifts for their kids. People hung out and wrapped presents

> A six-year-old girl told her parents that she didn't want her family to spend money on her birthday gifts this year. She asked instead that the money be given to Living Water International so that "other kids would have clean water to drink."

and played with kids so the parents could shop. As one person described it: "We felt it in the air that Christmas really can still change the world."

Believing that, we dreamed even bigger: What if we invited more faith communities to join us? We put together a few thousand dollars, launched a website, and invited others to join the Advent Conspiracy Jesus began so many years ago on a night in Bethlehem.

The story caught on, and people joined us. Hundreds of churches began to worship fully, spend less, give more, and love all. It became a movement that is still growing today. Churches all over the world are joining the Advent Conspiracy and discovering Jesus in a way that is changing lives. Entering the story was harder than we thought, more meaningful than we dared to dream, and one of the most beautiful encounters with Jesus that many of us have ever experienced.

Now tens of thousands of people all over the world are meeting the King born in a stable and serving his beloved, needy children. This book is about the prophetic dream birthed by the Advent of Jesus Christ—the dream that every Jesus follower would worship fully, spend less, give more, and courageously love all in the name and power of Jesus.

We refuse to be defined by our culture. Instead, emboldened by the Spirit, we are re-creating culture in the name of the good, the true, and the beautiful Jesus Christ.

A STORY, NOT A SYSTEM

The Advent Conspiracy is not a four-point checklist for how to do Christmas. It is not a formula or a fool-proof system to make your Christmas more meaningful.

The Advent Conspiracy is the story of the wondrous moment when God entered our world to make things right. It is the greatest story ever told, and it changes everything—including the way we celebrate Christmas.

As you read this book, understand what you're doing and why you're doing it. This is not about anger, disgust, or guilt—it is about entering the story of Jesus more deeply with a desire to worship more fully. It is not enough to say no to the way Christmas is celebrated by many; we need to say yes to a different way of celebrating.

Our dream is that as you read this book you will discover Christ and be transformed by entering his story. The idea is simple, yet sometimes it is simple ideas that change our lives in the best way possible.

"Since the inception of the Conspiracy, the entire Christmas offering that is collected during our multiple Christmas Eve services leaves our midst—no matter how much is given or where we are with the budget. This public commitment to worship Jesus by giving to the 'least of these' has changed us, and with God's help, the world."

The message of Jesus can still change the world. We continue to conspire together and discover new and creative ways in which Jesus can liberate the world. Will you write your life into his story? Will you join the prophetic dream?

[2]

THE RELIGION OF CONSUMERISM

Every day advertisements implore us to get more from life. Fulfillment is within our grasp—and we deserve it. Why wait when we can have everything now?

We can buy the house of our dreams with no money down. We can pull a fine bottle of French wine from our miniature wine cellar and savor the flavors while we sit on our suede sectional and watch our fifty-inch flat screen. Before going to sleep on our third new mattress in five years, we can go online to make our interest-only mortgage payment and order the kids some cheap Christmas gifts made in China—and something for ourselves, too, so we can get free shipping.

We have been told that this is the perfect life. We have a sense that when we get to this point, we will be satisfied. Yet if we spend our lives pursuing this dream, we discover that it cannot deliver on its grand promises of ease and satisfaction. There will always be a finer wine, a better television, a faster computer . . . and so the race goes on until the day we find ourselves surrounded by the latest and greatest of everything, yet feeling more alone and unhappy than ever before.

THE FASTEST-GROWING RELIGION IN THE WORLD

The fastest-growing religion in the world is not Islam or Christianity; the symbol of this rising faith is not the star and crescent or the cross, but a dollar sign. This expanding belief system is radical consumerism. It promises transcendence, power, pleasure, and fulfillment even as it demands complete devotion.

Many American Christians have decided they can, to put it bluntly, love both God and money. Our Scriptures tell how God's people were often intrigued by the promises of other gods, whether offering a bountiful harvest, sexual pleasure, or political power. God's people did not denounce him as they began to worship Baal or any other false god. Rather, they often continued to profess loyalty to God while they pursued their functional god. In the same way, American Christians have incorporated their devotion to consumerism with their Christian faith. Yet every step we make toward consumerism is one step farther off the path of Jesus the Liberating King.

It is now clear that the primary threat to true Christianity in America is consumerism—not liberalism, fundamentalism, Darwinism, secularism, or any other -ism that happens to achieve some level of influence and power.

Consumerism promises transcendence. Our consumer culture claims that the material thing we want most will elevate us above our current circumstances. A car, for example, is not simply a form of transportation; a car offers status, mystique, thrills, adventure, and confidence. If it were otherwise, we would all be driving the simplest, most cost-effective car available. Yet we buy cars for more than function, wondering which

[**An eighty-four-year-old grandmother apologized to her family for not being able to give lavish gifts on her limited income. This did not, however, keep her from giving $85 to the Advent Conspiracy Christmas offering.**]

model will be the best for us. These promises are not completely empty—for weeks or months we may wake up happier knowing that we will be driving the car of our dreams. Inside, however, we know this sort of happiness is fleeting, whether it ends in a crash or the slow creep of longing for an even better car.

The same is true of small purchases. Clothes protect our bodies from the weather and fit social norms. Yet most of us buy clothes to help us feel more attractive and successful. How many of us have ever put on a new outfit for a date or a fashionable suit for an interview?

In the religion of consumerism, the thing we desire becomes the symbol of whatever meaning it insinuates. Because we buy into the meaning, we believe we will become more significant, able to rise above the circumstances, frustrations, and mundane moments of our everyday lives. In short, our consumerism tells us that we'll be reborn.

Yet all too soon the luster starts to fade. We tell ourselves not to worry because there's another package to open, another order to place, or another catalog to flip through. Another messiah has come into our consumer world to save us from our self-created agony.

YOUR DISSATISFACTION IS GUARANTEED

Consumerism demands that we be dissatisfied. You will never hear a salesman say, "Great news! This is the last one of these you'll ever need to buy." We are constantly searching for the one thing that will satisfy us. Yet each time we trust the promises of our possessions, more barriers are raised between our true selves and God's plain command to love God above all things. It's not that we necessarily want more — it's that what we want is something we can't buy.

Consumerism can also poison our relationship with Christ. Jesus becomes a commodity we consume rather than a King who reigns. We tried Jesus. We were satisfied for six months, but then something about it just didn't meet our needs, and now we're ready to trade him in like a leased car for something better. Because we've been so deeply formed by a culture of consumerism, we cannot fathom the lasting value of Jesus.

Besides making false promises, consumerism detaches us from the human cost of the products we buy. Most of the time we have no idea how our shirt was made, who made it, or where it came from. It's practically magic: we can spend a few dollars and a new product travels across the world to our waiting arms.

Picture Fargo, North Dakota, in the dead of winter. Our detachment from what we consume allows us to buy and eat a delicious, ripe banana without thinking to ask where it came from or what its true cost might be. The religion of consumerism relies on our ignorance of its true workings.

Imagine picking out a shirt and hanging with the tag is a picture of the Guatemalan woman who earned thirty-three cents an hour sewing that shirt. There is no way any corporation is going to show us that picture because we might start calculating: "Wait . . . thirty-three cents an hour, twelve hours a day, six days a week . . . and they want forty bucks for the shirt?"[1]

Overhearing a conversation from one of his patients, a dentist asked about Advent Conspiracy. He was so moved by the story that he called AC asking if he could display its brochure at his office. Several of his patients told him they wanted to do Advent Conspiracy with their families.

No, consumerism requires our consciences to stay detached from the moral consequences of our purchases. We buy without thinking beyond the price and the promise of a newer, better self. Yet we ought not to deceive ourselves: this *is* a religion, and this *is* worship.

Sometimes uncovering the truth seems so overwhelming that we wonder if it's even worth beginning the search. It's much easier to once again bow down before the god of consumerism, to assume there's nothing we can do to make anything better. We keep playing the game and pretending everything is okay.

IS ANYONE OUT THERE?

Consumer greed and devotion is a snarling monster with razor-sharp teeth. It devours not only those from whom it takes, but also those who eagerly receive its plunder. James (the brother of Jesus) warns us of these dangers saying:

> *You have banked your lives on accumulating things, and* now you will watch your riches rot before your eyes

> as the moths devour your fine clothes. Your stockpile of silver and gold is tarnished and corroded: and this rust will stand up in the final judgment and testify against you. It will eat your flesh like fire *and become a permanent and painful reminder that* you have hoarded your wealth, *and it will not last* through these last days. Listen; *this is for you.* You held back a just wage from the laborers who mowed your fields, and that money is crying out against you, *demanding that justice be done.*[2]

Left unchecked, our constant striving for the next thing has fatal consequences. Our consumption all too easily becomes plundering and pillaging. "You'd better be on your guard," Jesus warned, "against any type of greed, for a person's life is not about having a lot of possessions."[3] Despite this caution, many of us still seem eager to give it a try.

LESS IS MORE

By definition, Christians believe that the most important gifts in the world are not the things we can see and touch. So what happens when we pursue material wealth? When we think of trouble, we tend to picture hardships and disease and accidents and domestic turmoil. Images of poverty and squalor and wretchedness may come to mind. Yet the real trouble we often face wears a very different mask.

In ancient times, God led the Israelites out of slavery, a brutal captivity during which their children had been euthanized, their work had been almost physically impossible, and they had lacked basic religious freedom. God intimidated their captors with terrifying plagues, parted the Red Sea to make possible their escape, and led them by pillars of cloud and fire to a good land he had promised them. On their journey to freedom, water burst from the rocks and manna rained daily from the sky.

How did the people respond to this remarkable provision? They complained: "We want meat!" "We're sick of this funky bread!" God, in his infinite wisdom, gave these ungrateful, murmuring people exactly what they asked for. "I'll give you meat," he said, "and you will eat it. Not for one day, ten days, or twenty—you will eat it until you vomit it out your nostrils."[4] Trouble in the form of *plenty*? You bet.

In these days it seems God has done the same for America: "You want wealth? I will give you obscene

> Three high school girls organized an initiative that raised awareness at their high school about the global water crisis. It all revolved around a single drop of water. From videos that played throughout lunch hour to a benefit concert to T-shirts that invited their fellow students to "be a drop out," they raised enough money for a well to be dug in West Africa.

wealth—and it will lead to your destruction." Ralph Winter, the founder of Frontier Mission Fellowship, writes: "The underdeveloped societies suffer from one set of diseases: tuberculosis, malnutrition, pneumonia, parasites, typhoid, cholera, typhus, etc. Affluent America has virtually invented a whole new set of diseases: obesity, arteriosclerosis, heart disease, stroke, lung cancer, venereal disease, cirrhosis of the liver, drug addiction, alcoholism.... In saving ourselves we have nearly lost ourselves."[5]

Consumerism's great risk is that we might get exactly what we want. What if, instead of pursuing the latest gadgets and most comfortable lifestyles, we became pilgrims like the Magi? What if we left behind our ease in order to witness—and worship—something infinitely better?

In our hearts we know that consumerism is not the Christian way to celebrate the birth of Christ. Could opting out of our cultural Christmas give us the chance to worship truly and love all? Might it be that the King of Kings is more powerful, and more worthy of our trust, than the god of consumerism? Are we willing to spend less and receive more?

[3]

WORSHIP FULLY

Our hearts are formed by what we worship. Excitement, anticipation, hope—each of these emotions swells around the object of our dearest affection. We spend our time and energy on what matters most to us.

What do we worship during Advent? "Jesus" is the right answer, of course, but is it the truthful answer? Does the way we spend our time, money, and energy testify that we worship God incarnate? Season after season, many churchgoers have learned to say the right things without allowing their words to reach their hearts. Simply saying that Jesus is the desire of our hearts doesn't make it truthful. In fact, saying the right things when they aren't believed things hinders true worship.

Looking honestly at the desires of our hearts is scarier than simply saying what people expect or demand.

Kids don't suffer from this fear. Ask a child what she is excited about at Christmas, and it's doubtful she'll exclaim with passion, "Jesus' birthday!" Before she's been indoctrinated with the proper religious mantra, she'll tell you about that shiny blue bike that she can't *wait* to ride on Christmas morning.

The things we desire are the things we worship. During Advent—a time of conspicuous consumption—we need to look closely at what we desire. Let's think beyond the well-rehearsed responses and strive to discover what is really in our hearts.

We spend billions of dollars during the holiday season, hoping—whether we admit it to ourselves or not—that the latest and greatest gift will fulfill us and those we give gifts to. We sprint through store after store, trying to find the perfect gift to express our love because we crave to be loved in return. We long for peace in place of the annual holiday family soap opera. We shop 'til we drop so we can finally rest. We go into debt and assume we're entitled to whatever we want.

We sit in church disconnected from the story because we know that deep inside we're too far from the stable to see much of anything.

The heart of what we're truly searching for—hope, peace, love, rest, worship—is in Christ, but each time we try to meet our desire for fulfillment at the mall, we take another step away from the nativity.

ENTER CHRISTMAS

The time of year when worshiping Jesus should be the easiest is often the hardest. The invitation to join the Advent Conspiracy is a call to remain in the gospel of Jesus and worship him—no matter how strongly the cultural demands of Christmas pull at us. The transformation initiated by Jesus is no different today than it was the day he was born—the source of joy, peace, and hope hasn't changed.

What if we could enter the story of Christ's coming in a fresh way? Read this father's account of how his young son began to experience Jesus at Christmas:

> My family had been talking about the birth of Christ and what it meant that God gave himself to be with us. I could see my children processing, but I didn't know if it was really connecting. But during an Advent worship service, my son brought his allowance savings without telling me. As our sanctuary filled with voices

celebrating the birth of Christ, we went forward to the communion table. Looking down at my son, I saw him put something like $40 into the offering for kids around the world. When I asked him about it later, he said he wanted to give like God had given to us.

Each year Advent brings another opportunity to worship Jesus in the miracle of his Incarnation, when God revealed himself to people in a new way. Nearly every character who encounters the infant King in the Advent story has the same response: worship. Their worship sprang from deep places of the heart that were touched for the first time by God-in-the-flesh. Such worship challenges old beliefs about God and what it means to be present with him.

THE INVITATION: MARY

Mary was a teenage girl engaged to marry a poor carpenter named Joseph. She lived on a dusty fringe of the mighty Roman Empire, just another powerless peasant in another insignificant town. Yet she was the young woman to whom God extended the invitation to be the mother of the Messiah, Jesus.

In Luke's account, Gabriel, God's archangel, announces

to Mary that she has found favor with God—she will give birth to a child, and she will name him Jesus. Mary's response—"Here I am, the Lord's humble servant. As you have said, let it be done to me"[1]—is as simple as it is inspiring. She doesn't protest or let her fear sway her from following God.

Mary joins the rich tradition of Jewish poets and prophets as she composes a song of devotion to her Lord:

> My soul glorifies the Lord
>   and my spirit rejoices in God my Savior,
> For he has been mindful
>   of the humble state of his servant.
> From now on all generations will call me blessed,
>   for the Mighty One has done great things for me—
>   holy is his name.
> His mercy extends to those who fear him,
>   from generation to generation.
> He has performed mighty deeds with his arm;
>   he has scattered those who are proud in their
>   innermost thoughts.
> He has brought down rulers from their thrones
>   but has lifted up the humble.
> He has filled the hungry with good things
>   but has sent the rich away empty.

He has helped his servant Israel,
remembering to be merciful
to Abraham and his descendants forever,
even as he said to our fathers.[2]

Mary's song is known as the Magnificat because she magnifies God, pointing to him as she worships and confesses his great love for and future salvation and deliverance of the oppressed.

We are not the humble lifted by God of whom Mary sings. We are the powerful, the rich, the self-absorbed. Hundreds of millions of people throughout the world live without clean water, housing, food, and education. These are the humble and hungry for whom Mary sings. Through her son, the Messiah, tyrants will be defeated and the oppressed will be liberated and ushered into a Kingdom that will have no end.

[One church put on their annual Christmas program, but this time rented out a local school and invited the homeless and teen moms, among other marginalized people. Over six hundred people attended and they ate, sang, and played together as one community.]

Mary announces that God is here! She carries God in her womb. The mystery of the moment is mind-bending. This Saving King is nothing less than her son and her God. Mary's worship begins with the ultimate paradox: a young girl, unwed and without power, influence, or wealth, cradles within her womb the divine power of the universe. The Creator who spoke creation into place is taking on fingers and toes inside her belly, and the One who holds all the wealth of the universe will soon nurse at her breast. Jesus is a fetus inside the worshiping Mary, who recognizes through grace that this great God is doing a great thing for all people!

How can we join Mary's Magnificat? Is the warm feeling we get when we sing "Silent Night" fitting worship for our King, or might Advent be about more than a happy holiday? What do we owe a God who entered our world to bring new life to his children? With Mary as our model, let poets pen odes, musicians compose songs, and prophets stand and call us to see what God sees: the birth of his Son signifies the beginning of the end of injustice.

Let our worship be an outpouring of our hearts. Let us take Jesus seriously and begin to desire the same things that move his heart. Let our worship drive us from the enclosure of church walls out into painful places to cry out for God's liberation. Author Mark Labberton puts it this way:

> This disparity between economics and justice is an issue of worship. According to the narrative of Scripture, the very heart of how we show and distinguish true worship from false worship is apparent in how we respond to the poor, the oppressed, the neglected, and the forgotten. As of now, I do not see this theme troubling the waters of worship in the American church. But justice and mercy are not add-ons to worship, nor are they the consequences of worship. Justice and mercy are intrinsic to God and therefore intrinsic to the worship of God.[3]

A HOLY DRAMA: JOSEPH

Joseph, the earthly father of Jesus, has a problem. His fiancée is pregnant, and the baby isn't his. In Joseph's

> "A seventh grade girl's parents who are of a different faith gave generously to AC because of the amazing way our church is involved in AC as well as in their daughter's life."

world, this was beyond taboo. Though Joseph could have exposed Mary to public shame and punishment, he decides to break off the engagement and let things end as quietly as possible.

That's when the angel shows up. In a dream, God's messenger tells Joseph not to break his pledge to Mary, because her baby was conceived by the Holy Spirit. He will be called Jesus, meaning our "Salvation" or "God to the rescue." Matthew's gospel points to the prophet Isaiah: "The virgin will be with child and will give birth to a son, and they will call him Immanuel"—which means, "God with us."[4]

God came in person to walk with us, as one of us, to save us. God entered into the very situation he wants to heal.

When we worship Jesus at Christmas, we're reminded that God came for all humanity. No matter our momentary circumstances, every human needs to be rescued from sin by the Son. We in the West, in particular, need to be rescued from our own self-centered agendas, from the fact that we become bored with "God-with-us," Immanuel.

Joseph chose obedience. However scared he was of the ramifications, he still took Mary home to be his wife. He was a fool—a holy fool who gave up his reputation and rights because of a call from God.

One of the common fears people have about the Advent Conspiracy is what their relatives might think, do, feel, or say. Quite honestly, in this day and time, it does sound crazy at first to spend less, to give more, and to use our holiday money to love our brothers and sisters around the world. Joseph, however, reminds us that while the call of God isn't always easy or conventional, it is always right—and God will give us the courage to follow if we are willing to obey. Like Joseph, when we act in obedience to God's invitation—despite even the social cost—we help God's will be done on earth as it is in heaven.

RESPONDING TO THE CALL: THE SHEPHERDS

Another of God's angelic messengers brought the news of Jesus' birth to shepherds working nearby. At that time, shepherds were often despised as thieves unfit for more respectable occupations. Their testimony was not allowed in court nor their presence in polite society, so shepherds found their place on the outskirts of towns. They were largely shunned by the mainstream population.

Yet we are loved by a God who sees the overlooked. He looks at our hearts, not our place in society. So at the birth of his only Son, God chose a group of people invisible to most of the world to celebrate the good news of their Savior's birth. After hearing from God, the shepherds immediately went to witness the miracle for themselves, after which they spread the glorious news far and wide.

Are we willing to respond to this call to leave our responsibilities and hurry off to see this miracle? To pause long enough to look upon the Savior who is Christ the Lord? Will we miss the invitation?

Long after the angels left, the shepherds continued to worship. Communities that have joined the Advent Conspiracy have had similar experiences. We may not have seen the angelic host that awed the shepherds, but we are experiencing a sustainable worship that transcends the season of Christmas. The good news of the birth of Jesus moves into a world that needs him in every season.

Doug and Vania Moore, a couple from Imago Dei Community in Portland, Oregon, reimagined their wedding in light of the Advent story:

> We participated in Advent Conspiracy for two years, and we deeply believed in the value of celebrating the Advent season by worshiping Christ through the relational activity and giving our time and resources to those in need. When it came time to plan our wedding day, we realized the wedding industry was commercialized much like Christmas—the average American wedding costs $27,000! We asked ourselves, "Does celebrating our marriage require us to accrue large amounts of debt, or would God desire the emphasis to be placed elsewhere?"
>
> The answer we came to was the same answer we discovered through entering the story of Advent: God desires this to be a fundamentally *relational* event rather than a *consumer* event. Pursuing our own "Covenant Conspiracy," we chose to build the wedding around worshiping God and celebrating our relationships with friends and family. We intentionally limited the amount of money we spent. We asked our guests to take the money they would have spent on wedding gifts and give that money to Living Water International. Over $2,500 was given to help build wells around the world, while the entire wedding and reception cost less than $2,000.

> Just as we experienced Christ during Advent, we found great joy in celebrating relationships and giving to "the least of these" — a greater joy by far than if we had simply followed the story our culture is telling us.

Living out our worship in tangible ways begins here and becomes the way we are invited to live and breathe in the glorious, ordinary moments of our lives.

FROM A GREAT DISTANCE: THE WISE MEN

The Magi were scholars and astrologers from Persia and Babylon, east of Judea. After noticing a change in the star patterns in the sky, they began the long and arduous journey to Jerusalem, looking for the one the ancient texts foretold would be born King of the Jews.

The reigning king was Herod the Great. Although not a Jewish king, he had gained power through political marriages and carefully cultivated friendships with influential Romans. Herod protected his empire with military might, bribery, and violent acts that extended even to members of his own family.

The Magi must have been people of some influence

because they were given an audience with the king. They had the courage to ask Herod for directions to where the one true King was to be born so they could worship him.

Jesus' kingly inauguration stands in contrast with Herod's tyranny—and that of the surrounding empires. Herod's citizens were controlled by military power, financial strength, and technological development. But Jesus' Kingdom rises up differently. Jesus reveals his Kingdom in vulnerability, solidarity with the poor, and self-sacrifice—far from the worldly power of Herod's world.

Which king is worthy of our worship?

When the Magi finally came to the place where Jesus and his parents were living, they offered him costly gifts. These men were not playing the worship games of which many of us are guilty—these gifts of gold and precious spices nearly cost the Magi their lives before Herod.

Our worship must be reborn. The wise men show us what happens when someone glimpses the true worthiness of Christ. We will travel across the world to meet him, confront dominant world systems, and give our all for our King.

THE STORY THAT CHANGES THE WORLD

It has been beautiful to see people in our communities worship in a similar way. Whoever we are and wherever we find ourselves, we are learning to worship with the wise men, traveling across the world to bring the gift of ourselves—our presence, our labor, our money, our love—to hungry, thirsty, sick people who need Jesus.

Our eyes are being opened. The empire that we have been fueling with our time, attention, and money is not the Kingdom of Jesus. What might happen if, at Advent and throughout the year, all of God's people worshiped like the Magi? What transformation would occur as God's people moved across the globe loving Jesus with our time, attention, and money?

The characters of the Advent drama are all threads in a rich, textured tapestry of worship. It is a story that is still unfolding, that still inspires action. A story about the radical solidarity of Jesus worshipers who commit themselves to standing with the least of these in the far corners of the world and in the midst of injustice. A story about passionate resistance from people who refuse to be enveloped by another empire's demands and instead live simply and faithfully for their King. A story about faithful worship at the feet of a glorified and yet humble King.

As followers of Jesus, our options are clear: we can inhabit the story of a corrupt world, or we can enter the story of God through Christ.

If we choose the former, we need not change anything. Christmas—and the rest of our lives—will look much the same as now. But if we choose to enter the story of God, we choose to enter the greatest story ever, the story that changes everything. When we enter the Advent story, we cannot remain silent!

> "Dear Pastor: If you don't get this message, then call me. I am going to ask for some money and toys from Santa (for other kids). I'm going to ask Santa to also send food and water to those kids. I also have my own bucket of money to give them." (letter from a five-year-old)

Like Mary, we will sing to our redeeming God. Like Joseph, we will obey without regard to the cost. Like the shepherds, we will leave our busyness to worship Christ. Like the Magi, we will confront anything that stands in the way of our worship, whether worldly empires or our own fears.

We will celebrate, sing, dance, pray, meditate, and love our way into a story that is of great joy for all people. Christmas changed the world the day Jesus was born in a cold, dark stable; Christmas will change the world again.

[4]

SPEND LESS

We have inserted ourselves into Jesus' birth story and opened our hearts to the possibility of a deeper, fuller worship experience—not only at Christmas, but beyond. Jesus has become the reason for our season. Given that later in his ministry, Jesus said, "People try to serve both God and money—but you can't. *You must choose one or the other,*"[1] how do we turn the tables? We may be face to face with a newborn Jesus who brings us to our knees in worship, but spending less at Christmas may still seem like an impossibly hard next step.

Christmas is a season of excess. It is difficult to walk against the crowd that seems to want nothing more than to "eat, drink, and be merry." Spending less requires us to plan, research, and cultivate relationships—pursuits that are more taxing than flipping through the latest catalog or bingeing at the mall.

However, as we choose to go against the cultural flow, it is important to remember that spending less on Christmas presents doesn't mean we love our friends and family any less. In fact, we will often find that those to whom we give creative, personal gifts will see our love—and perhaps God's—more clearly than ever before.

GIVING BEAUTIFULLY

"Spend less" is ambiguous. Spend less than last year? Spend less than my neighbor? Spend less than the average American, who spends one thousand dollars on Christmas gifts? Yes and no.

The key is to ask the question and be willing to engage the emerging tensions. How much is too much? How can you tell when you have too much? Who determines what you "need"? The line between excessive wealth and simplicity may be hard to find—but it's hard to escape the conclusion that nearly all of us have too much.

Begin by asking a few simple questions. For instance, how many coats do I need? John the Baptist says if you have two coats then you should give the second away. I wonder—and maybe rationalize—did he mean two coats of the same style or purpose? I have a raincoat, a ski jacket, a leather coat, an overcoat, a windbreaker, multiple sport coats, a light coat, and a heavy coat, and I may have a few others.

The challenge is to balance our desires with the needs in our communities and the rest of the world. This means that shopping will become less about entertainment and more about necessities. It means that researching purchases may become more complicated than simply seeking the greatest value or the highest visibility.

What about community consequences? Are you supporting businesses that treat their employees well or advocate for causes that you believe in? Do you agree with the ways the product is advertised? Are they using sexual appeal to sell the product? Do children see these advertisements?

What about environmental consequences? Was your television manufactured in an area where

> A family agreed to not exchange presents and instead gave that money to a charity or cause of their own choosing. On Christmas Day, the time around the tree was spent listening as each person described their gift and why that cause mattered to them.

factories routinely ignore environmental guidelines? Is the product recyclable or reusable? Was the product shipped halfway across the globe? If so, the environmental cost is significant.

We must also ask what story we are telling our children. Is it healthy to give our children whatever they want? Does it build character? Many of us are guilty of giving our children too much. Many children are completely overwhelmed with gifts, the sheer volume of which distracts them from the celebration of Jesus. The Cherry family in Austin, Texas, chose to radically change the way they experience Christmas, and the first step was slashing their spending budget. They were nervous and unsure how their children would respond, but the true beauty of Christmas changed them. They described their new way of giving this way:

> When we first talked with the boys about changing our Christmas budget, they were a little disappointed. But looking back, I don't remember seeing any of that on Christmas Day. David and I are so grateful for Advent Conspiracy. We knew things didn't feel right, that there was something askew with our Christmases—but we couldn't pinpoint exactly what was wrong. I remember thinking something must be missing. Maybe there was something more.... Now I know that more for us actually means a whole lot less.

Christmas in America is more about getting what we want than giving what people need. Is this the tradition we want to pass down to our children?

IS SPENDING LESS WRONG?

Perhaps you've heard something like this: "Surely you don't really want Americans to spend less; you must understand that our economy relies on consumer spending. If Americans do not spend, then Americans will ultimately lose their jobs and suffer. Do you really want to cause suffering by asking Christians to spend less?"

At first glance, this circular argument seems to make

sense. However, spending less does not mean spending nothing. Rather, we strive to thoughtfully evaluate what we support with our spending and allow our spending to support products, people, and causes that are worthy of being supported.

SPEND LESS, EXCEPT WHEN YOU SHOULD SPEND MORE

Suppose you have a twenty-seven-inch television. Do you need a new forty-two-inch television to help you celebrate the birth of Christ? Do we need to spend more on products we don't need, especially products whose hidden personal, communal, and environmental costs are so high?

Yet sometimes we purchase something in order to keep someone employed. In a desperately poor Calcutta slum where young women are often forced to become sex workers because they lack any other options, a new business is blossoming that teaches these young girls to make beautiful handmade journals. Suppose you already have a journal. Do you need to buy yourself three new journals handmade by former prostitutes in Calcutta? Will that help you celebrate the birth of

Christ? You might choose to buy a box of journals, but it becomes more about the girls than the journals themselves. We spend less at Christmas, except when we should spend more.

A pastor in a Buenos Aires shantytown where homes are little more than mud huts gets his church members to make thousands of gorgeous leather Bible covers that are sold in America and used to support these indigenes in Argentina. Most Americans may not need a new Bible cover, but when we choose to purchase one, we can be grateful knowing that God is using our money for the greater good of his Kingdom.

There are times we will want to spend more to help others keep gainful employment, feed their children, and get basic medical care. The question we must ask as we spend is, Who is our money supporting? Do we want our Christmas spending to support slavery or child labor or the buildup of the Chinese military? If not, we will be careful about buying any chocolate products, unless they are certified as Fair Trade, or any toy made in China. Do we want to support corporations that exploit workers in sweatshops and pay them less than a living wage? If not, we'll avoid most of the stores at the mall. Do we want our Christmas spending to pollute the earth that God created and calls us to preserve and care for?

Asking questions like these helps us eliminate spending from our budgets that brings harm to ourselves, our neighbors, or our world.

THE PROBLEM IS NOT CAPITALISM

It is possible to spend compassionately and responsibly regardless of our economic system. When capitalism unwittingly marries unbridled Western individualism, however, catastrophe results. In such a cultural system, every person creates a society of one, making a mockery of the idea of a nation of liberty and freedom. The thinking behind such a warped worldview goes something like this: "If in my freedom I make choices based solely on value or convenience, I shouldn't feel guilty. It's my right, and it's the American way." But some of those choices may devastate the lives of hundreds or even thousands of people.

How strange and sad it is that debt and consumerism reach their pinnacle on the morning we celebrate the birth of Jesus—the Savior who came to liberate us from these things. When we give gifts without regard to "the least of these," it reflects an American brand of capitalism gone wrong.

The Creator of heaven and earth had something very different in mind for his creation. The Bible tells us to approach life and finances with an open hand: "The objective is not to go under so others will have some relief; the objective is to use this opportunity today to supply their needs out of your abundance. *One day it may be the other way around,* and they will need to supply your needs from what they have. That's equality."[2]

THE LOVE OF MONEY

The love of money, which the apostle Paul called "the root of all sorts of evil,"[3] plagues all people, even (and sometimes especially) people of faith. Televangelists want more satellites; pastors and rabbis and imams want bigger houses of worship. We want bigger cars, homes, and a corner office with a view. Why should we who happen to profess faith be any different? Why should we spend less and give more?

In the first century, the apostle Paul employed pointed rhetoric to warn his friends about excess: "But those who chase riches are constantly falling into temptation and snares. They are regularly caught by their own stupid and harmful desires, dragged down and pulled under into ruin and destruction."[4] Some theologians and pastors try to justify financial excess as a blessing from God. They crave God's stamp of approval on their chosen lifestyles and view their abundance as a reward for personal righteousness. They think, "If God doesn't like what he sees, why did he gift me so richly?"

The "infectious greed" that Alan Greenspan railed against in Congress cannot be eliminated through rivers of new legislation flowing out of Washington. Our economy and our society have accepted radical greed as the norm, and each of us somehow justifies the suffering of others that our lifestyle causes. The only

An owner of a private truck line established an optional payroll deduction program with his fifteen employees. He matches their deductions with all proceeds forwarded to Living Water International.

sure remedy is a change of heart, and the best place to begin is at the feet of the newborn Jesus.

Are we willing to rethink the way we use our wealth? Do we long to rediscover the beauty of true giving? The Judeo-Christian tradition offers clear direction about what we willingly offer back to God to use for his greater purposes. The Hebrew Scriptures talk a great deal about giving a tithe (10 percent of income), while the New Testament opens the floodgates and pushes us toward boundary-busting generosity. Reflecting on the meaning of God's gifts to us, the apostle Paul says, "You will be made rich in everything so that your generosity *will spill over in every direction.*"[5]

An Advent Conspiracy pastor in Pennsylvania experienced this in his congregation: "People in our church grabbed hold of the concept of spending less. People made Christmas simpler in order to worship fully. People gave relationally. A woman chose to ask her neighbors what their favorite charities were, and instead of giving them a typical gift, she donated to those agencies in their names. Christmas is becoming something different—and something better!"

Like Jesus, the twentieth-century author C. S. Lewis

believed that the best way to break money's power is to give it away—yet he shrank from suggesting a rigid formula for giving. He wrote:

> I do not believe one can settle how much we ought to give. I am afraid the only safe rule is to give more than we can spare. In other words, if our expenditure on comforts, luxuries, amusements, etc., is up to the standard common among those with the same income as our own, we are probably giving away too little. If our charities do not at all pinch or hamper us, I should say they are too small. There ought to be things we should like to do and cannot do because our charitable expenditure excludes them.[6]

What would our world look like if people of faith began acting on Lewis's suggestion? What would happen in our nation if both executives and laborers began practicing a kind of generosity that "pinched"? How would our neighborhoods be transformed if we gave more than we could spare? This Advent season, what would it take for us to actually give it a try?

At the end of the day we hope that your celebration of the birth of the Liberating King is focused less on what you spend and more on giving from a place of true worship.

A FEW IDEAS TO CONSIDER

- Be considerate when spending money.
- Set your budget; know your limit (if it's early enough, start saving for a debt-free celebration).
- Before you start buying, consider each person on your list. Think about your relationship and what significance it brings to your life.
- Consider your core values and whether what you are buying reflects those values.
- Consider drawing names, giving one less gift than last year (or maybe two).

[5]

GIVE MORE

This invitation to push back against overspending and overconsumption during Advent resonates deeply with people of various backgrounds and economic realities. We've grown weary of the holiday ad campaigns that seem to start earlier and earlier each year. Kids struggle to find the connection between their Christmas wish list and the story of Jesus' birth. Parents search for even a fleeting moment of worship. Many of us reach the end of each Advent season with an aching emptiness. Sifting through piles of things we don't need and may never use, something deep inside tells us we missed it —whatever it is our soul longs for this time of year.

And now, when we're invited to rebel against some of this craziness by spending less, it simply seems right. But then we're being encouraged to give more? That sure sounds like a contradiction, doesn't it?

Maybe not.

We can all agree that there is still something deeply moving and beautiful about certain gifts. Think about the most memorable Christmas present you've ever received. What was it that touched you? Why do you still remember it to this day? You probably aren't remembering a pair of new cars sitting in the driveway with big red bows on top or a huge diamond bracelet hanging on the tree. For most of us, the special gift we best remember is a different kind of gift—a relational gift.

The best gifts celebrate a relationship. The reason a father keeps a simple frame with a picture of his girls glued in the middle isn't because it's an expensive work of art. It's because his daughters gave that gift specifically to him, and they created it with their own energy. When that father looks at that particular gift, he's reminded of two girls who love him and a relationship that he's still celebrating.

It sounds so obvious, yet we seem to have drifted from this liberating, straightforward truth: the Father gave his one and only Son. God's answer for the world's problems has never been material things. God did not give us more stuff — even good stuff like work, food, or health. He gave us himself.

This simple truth is why giving is still a good way to celebrate the birth of Jesus. It also points to a way out of the chaos of consumerism that Christmas has become, taking us back to the joy that can still be found at the heart of this story. Our giving can actually reflect in some small way the power and beauty of God coming into our world as one of us.

THE INCARNATION

Incarnation is a word that doesn't even show up in our Bibles, but the writers of Scripture describe it so powerfully that we cannot deny its reality. The Incarnation is the moment when Jesus, the divine Son of the Eternal Father, entered our story as a human baby. Only someone with an especially large ideological axe to grind would attempt to deny the existence of a man named Jesus who lived in Palestine two thousand years ago. And while this is certainly an important aspect of the Incarnation — that Jesus lived on this earth as a human — we know it means more than a simple historical fact.

The miracle of Christmas is the infinite becoming finite —an infant fully human and still fully God. This profound truth lies at the heart of the historic Christian faith. It unites Catholics and Protestants, Baptists and Episcopalians, house churches and megachurches. All Christians confess that Jesus is God. While we could refer to famous church councils in the centuries that followed his time on earth or quote from the creeds of our faith, this truth was declared much earlier.

The gospel of John begins with this sentence: "In the beginning was the Word"—John's term for his friend Jesus in these opening lines to this eyewitness account—"and the Word was with God, and the Word was God. He was with God in the beginning. Through him all things were made; without him nothing was made that has been made."[1] John tells us Jesus not only made us, he also formed the world around us and cast the planets around that world and spaced out the galaxies beyond those planets.

Unfortunately, these familiar words have grown stale to many. We seem to rush past the mind-stretching claims being made in this opening paragraph—and when we do, we miss the power of John's words. Listen to the same verses from a different translation that is still faithful to the original text: "Before time itself was measured, the Voice was speaking. The Voice was and is God. This *celestial* Voice remained ever present with the Creator; His speech shaped the entire cosmos."[2] That's who Jesus is—the one whose speech shaped the entire cosmos. John has no problem telling us that Jesus of Nazareth is more than a gifted rabbi and good friend. Jesus is more than an extraordinary human being—Jesus was and is the Son of God.

So when we read a few verses later that "the Word became flesh and made his dwelling among us,"[3] we understand that to be the miracle of the Incarnation. John is unambiguous. When he writes of the Word becoming flesh, it means just what we think it means. God became bone and skin and guts. It's not just that Jesus is God—it's that Jesus, as God, chose to become one of us. That's the Incarnation. The one who spoke galaxies into existence, in the words of author Alan Hirsch, "moved into our neighborhood in an act of humble love the likes of which the world has never known."[4]

Jesus as the Incarnation of God is our fullest and best understanding of God. Jesus himself said, "The Father and I are one"[5] and that when we've seen him, we've seen the Father.[6] What does all this mean? Because of the Incarnation, the infinite God becomes more tangible, more approachable, and more (though never completely) comprehensible. It's because of Jesus that we know who the Eternal God of the universe is and what he's really like. Talk about a relational gift! But it gets even better.

THE STORY HAS FOREVER CHANGED

The Incarnation is what we celebrate when we gather for worship. It's what we celebrate at the communion table. It's the very good news we proclaim to a world that has forgotten what very good news sounds like. God was here in flesh and blood as the fulfillment of a promise—and that gives us real hope. In the strong words of theologian Tom Wright, "Jesus exploded into the life of ancient Israel—the life of the whole world, in fact—not as a teacher of timeless truths, nor as a great moral example, but as the one through whose life, death, and resurrection God's rescue operation was put into effect, and the cosmos turned its great corner at last."[7] Apart from the Incarnation, we would never fully know the depths to which we are loved or the lengths to which God can be trusted. That's what we celebrate each Christmas.

When we give relationally during the Advent season, this is what we remember: it's an opportunity to worship as we remind each other of the gift that was given for our sake.

GETTING STARTED

Let's face it: one of the big pressures each Christmas season is coming up with gift ideas. And for some, that pressure seems to increase when we decide not to stop at the mall and buy Uncle Murray that sweater he was never going to wear anyway. Now we have to be creative. Now we have to think. And it's usually about now that some of us get a little fearful that we're not going to come up with anything meaningful. So where do we start? While there are resources available which allow co-conspirators around the world to share ideas,[8] let's begin by again taking our cue from the story of Jesus.

As others have pointed out, the Incarnation suggests, in very practical terms, what it means to give ourselves to one another.[9] Let's quickly look at three aspects of what happened when God gave us his one and only Son.

God gave us his presence.

In the Incarnation, God drew close in a very specific, historical way. In Matthew's account of Jesus' birth, he takes us back to the words of Isaiah, stating "They will call him Immanuel."[10] He then explains that this is a Hebrew name that means "God with us." Many of us remember to repeat this name at Christmas each year and tell each other what it means—but do we allow it to permeate the way we live during the Advent season? Is it possible that even our gift-giving could be drenched with this beautiful moment when God gave us his presence in a unique, flesh-and-blood way? The apostle Paul writes that Jesus is the image of the invisible God.[11] God had a face and a voice and he lived with real people. There's something incredibly tangible about God's gift. What can that teach us about the way we give Christmas gifts?

Our world is increasingly fractured, yet we often mask the distance this causes with a kind of pseudo-community—we call, we email, we text, we Facebook, we Tweet, and the list goes on. These can be important ways to keep in touch, but they can never replace the flesh-and-blood aspect of a relationship. We need to be *with* each other. To hear another voice, to see another face, to hold another

> A father was walking by his family's Christmas tree one morning when he noticed a water bottle stuffed with coins and dollar bills. When he asked his six-year-old about it, his son told him that he had taken the water bottle to school and told his classmates about AC and facts about the water problem around the world. The best part is his parents never even knew he had done this.

hand ... it's one of the ways we are reminded that we are not alone.

When we make time to be with someone, it's a gift—a relational gift. The conscious giving of our time and presence to another is not a new concept, but it is a neglected one. Consider how you can creatively express to that friend or family member how much you want to *be* with them.

Picture the following scenario: A young man buys his father a pound of coffee beans with one stipulation: *Dad can only enjoy this gift with his grown son.* And in the hours and days it will take to drink those cups of coffee, that son just wants to listen to his dad tell stories as the two of them get reacquainted. What does that say to this father? He hears from his son: "I want to spend time with you and discover how you became the man that you are." This is what it means to give your presence in simple, but meaningful ways.

The gift of Jesus was personal.

Luke's account of the Christmas story includes that very famous angelic announcement: "Today, in the city of David, a Liberator has been born for you! He is the promised Liberating King, the Supreme Authority!"[12] A Savior has been born for *you*—a very personal gift! Over and over the Gospels demonstrate the relational nature of Jesus. He simply liked being with people.

Not only that, he intentionally cultivated those relationships. He paid attention. He listened. He noticed. He did everything that people in a hurry forget to do.

We've all received gifts that were, shall we say, less than personal (feel free to insert your own awkward example here). But the truth is, we've given gifts like that too. Generic disposable gifts are not only a waste of money, they practically scream, "I haven't thought about you in a long time, but I still felt obligated to give you something." Is that kind of giving moving us any closer to celebrating the story of Jesus?

Relational giving means that we pay attention to the other person. We think about who they are and what they care about.

A father and his teenage daughter were enjoying their last Christmas at home before she headed off to college that summer. For him, the days were beginning to blur into weeks and the little girl he was bouncing on his lap just yesterday was going to leave tomorrow.

What did that father give his daughter that Christmas? Two beautiful blank journals with these instructions: she was to fill one, and he'd fill the other. During the next year, which would include her final days of high school, an all-too-brief summer, and her first semester away from home, they both committed to writing: thoughts about leaving home, questions and fears, frustrations with overprotective parenting, what it meant to let go, and how it feels to watch your child become an adult. The next Christmas, they'd exchange their journals.

Two empty journals for Christmas—that's what a daughter got from her dad? How impersonal such a gesture might appear at first glance—and how inadequate! But no gift could have been more relational, more personal, and no other gift would stand a chance of being appreciated so warmly or remembered for so long.

His gift was costly.

There is an aspect of the Incarnation that is God becoming a servant. In places like the book of Philippians, we see that Jesus intentionally took on the form of a servant.[13] He did not force his way into our world as the powerful King he truly is. Instead, Jesus chose to enter the story in the humblest of ways. As Hirsch reminds us, "This [truth] now commits us to servanthood and humility in our relationships with each other and the world."[14]

Of course, his humility did not stop there, for it led to the cross. In the words of Jesus himself, "Even the Son of Man came not to be served but to be a servant—to offer His life as a ransom for others."[15]

The gift God gave us cost him everything. What does that mean for us as we now give to one another?

In practical terms, it means we must accept that

relational giving will cost us. While not to the depths of what it cost Jesus to become human, much less the sacrifice of the cross, relational gifts will cost our time and energy. It would be easier to stop by the store or go online to buy something "in the ballpark."

Relational giving will also be risky, at times. What if they don't like it? What if they don't understand our intent? What if they don't appreciate the time we put into expressing love for them? This, too, is a reflection of the Incarnation. Didn't Jesus give himself knowing full well that some would reject or misunderstand him? We ought not to take this too far, or we'll succumb to the martyr complex that lurks just beneath the surface in many well-intentioned Christians. But part of relational giving is understanding that our heartfelt gifts simply might not be appreciated. Hopefully they will be, though, as often even the crustiest of hearts will soften with such personal gestures.

But the gift is not about the giver, but about the other. Such gifts, when given with this spirit of humility, drip with grace. Can you think of a better way to celebrate Jesus?

Consider a woman who, without her friend knowing

> Two local churches partnered to rescue several refugees in Rwanda who needed only bus fare to escape to Nairobi and relative safety. What seemed like an insurmountable amount ($55 per person) was little more than what some in the group spent on diet soda each month. Within days, the money was collected. Within weeks, the refugees were out of Rwanda. According to their new church in Nairobi, these rescued ones have injected new life into their worship services with their loud and grateful singing.

it, asked this person's friends and family to each write a note or send a picture that celebrated that one beautiful life. Over the course of weeks, she began compiling a scrapbook with these photos, drawings, notes, letters, and poems of various lengths. Sometimes it took some friendly reminders to encourage participation. On Christmas Day, the gift was truly a work of art. It was beautiful, of course, but the contents of this multi-layered gift took much longer to truly appreciate. Imagine the tears of joy, the sometimes bittersweet memories, and the reflections of a life well-lived as this friend slowly went through the book page by page on Christmas morning.

Here's the last detail: the woman who had assembled this whole project wasn't even there when her friend opened it! She thought it best for such a gift to be enjoyed in the privacy of family, so she asked them to present the gift on her behalf Christmas morning. There was no moment of triumph, no basking in the glory of her very generous gesture. For her, it really wasn't about that. It was a gift of love given in the spirit of her Savior, who is himself a servant.

If we can resist the trap of giving easy gifts, and if we can reject the assumption that giving expensive gifts or many gifts is the best way to express love, something else might begin to happen. We might experience moments of relational giving that our friends and family will care about and remember. Our kids will learn what it means to give gifts that are personal and meaningful. Our neighbors and coworkers and friends will watch us celebrate Christmas differently, and they'll hear the good news loud and clear through the seasonal static.

[6]

LOVE ALL

When the Advent Conspiracy was taking shape, some of us were part of a strategic team that was assessing the water crisis in Liberia. The handful of churches that first caught the vision of what could happen if we celebrated Christmas differently were committed to funneling some of our resources away from overconsumption and toward those who might be considered the "least of these" around the world.

Sensing that our five churches could start to make a difference, we journeyed to Africa with a team from Living Water International, a nonprofit that digs freshwater wells in places around the world most of us don't know exist. At times, it didn't seem like we'd be able to reach some of these villages. Bouncing from rut to rut for hours in the back of a Land Rover made us painfully aware how far removed we are from the struggles of many in this world.

> A South African church threw a Christmas party at a local school for the underprivileged and gave 750 children gifts that they had specifically asked for. The church members' children came along and celebrated alongside them.

We stopped at a village that, like many others, welcomed us with beautiful smiles and open arms. We were led through tall grasses, away from the village, to what they referred to as their "well." If it was a well, it was not like any well we'd ever seen. It sat next to a swamp that leached untold disease into the water from which families drew their water every day. This stagnant, gray-green pool infested with insects was all these people had. Even as we talked with the village elders, women would casually brush away the film that clung to the top of this water as they filled their pots.

Is this the dead and stagnant water from "broken cisterns"[1] that the prophet Jeremiah warned about? Looking at this water dripping with disease, it seemed all too real. Surely God was leading us. Not only could we push back against the hyper-consumerism of our own culture, we could also begin to heal the disease that was seeping into this one. And as a result, we could share the story of Jesus, the Living Water. Everything seemed to be coming together in this one moment.

We listened as the village chief told us of those who had died recently because of illnesses that came from drinking this water. Standing with us in our small circle was a man whose son had just died from a waterborne disease. The faces of these elders were somber and hopeless, almost resigned to the fact that burying their children would always be a part of their lives.

We knew that in several weeks our churches would be taking Christmas offerings. We knew that by partnering with Living Water International, in a couple of months, this village would not have to rely on that well ever again. For us, this was good news and we wanted to share it with the chief and his elders.

When this message of hope was delivered—with great passion by a translator from the area who was as excited as we were—the weathered face of this honorable elder remained impassive. He simply stared at us.

Even our translator was puzzled by this lack of

emotion. When he asked the chief if he understood what this would mean for his people, the answer was unforgettable: "Others have made promises in the name of this Jesus, but they were never kept." Here was a man whose hope had dried up and blown away because others had made promises in the name of Jesus that they'd never bothered to keep.

THE REACTION SAYS IT ALL

Somewhere along the way, this man and his village were probably "told the right things" about Jesus: how God loved the world so much that he gave his only Son. Apparently, they were also told by well-meaning Christians that help was on the way, that someone had noticed their struggle. But no one showed up. Nothing changed. Kids were still dying in the village, and the name of Jesus had been dragged through the mud.

Is it possible that someone thought it would be enough to tell the people of this village that God loved them without feeling compelled to be an active agent of God's love? Sometimes we are so focused on what happens after people die that we don't pay attention to the life they're living now. Author Scot McKnight warns us that the church suffers when it treats humans as souls made for eternity instead of whole persons made for now *and* eternity.[2] Of course, it's not just the church that suffers—it's everyone who might have been helped by a church intent on participating in God's plan to bring justice and hope to this world. When Jesus said he came to bring good news to the poor, he meant it.[3]

Jesus was more than an activist, however. Ready to save people's bodies now *and* for eternity, Jesus taught us to pray for daily bread and for our sins to be forgiven. When he spoke of the poor in the gospel of Luke, there was a deeper, spiritual meaning.[4] The good news of the Kingdom is for anyone in dire need of God—even those who might assume they'll never be helped. Soldiers, beggars, the religious elite, tax collectors, rich people, prostitutes, the working class, lepers—Jesus brought good news to everyone.

THE HEART OF THE CHRISTMAS STORY

God came to the poor—in other words, to each of us. The apostle Paul reminds us that "[Jesus] set aside His infinite riches and was born into the lowest circumstance so that you may gain great riches through His humble poverty."[5]

What does this mean? Jesus gave up the glory of heaven to be born into a sin-scarred world. That glorious night in Bethlehem, every day of his life, and in the deadly pain of the cross, Jesus became poor for our sake. Jesus entered our poverty so we would no longer be poor. The priceless gift of a restored relationship with God and others is now offered to those who could never afford it. The outrageous wealth of his righteousness is credited to those who don't deserve it. To those of us who are poor, this is very good news.

But is it still relevant news? Can Christmas still change the world? We're discovering that the answer is a resounding yes! But how exactly does that happen? How can Christmas and the way we celebrate it still change the world?

As poor people who have met with the righteous wealth of God, it is now our turn to model his generosity by sharing our wealth with those in need. Christmas is our chance to move closer to those in crisis, not further away. It is our time to notice those who are normally ignored. In short, it is our turn to love as we have been loved. In practical terms, our love must include caring for the poor in our midst.

Over and over we see Jesus teaching that God is on the side of the impoverished, even when no one else is. Throughout the Gospels, he raises the status of those the world mistreats and marginalizes—people who are deemed hopeless and beyond help. Jesus is clear: he expects his followers to do the same.

There's no way around it: Jesus calls us to love and care for the poor.

At Christmas, one of the things that should distinguish a Christ-follower is a love that reaches out to the hungry and thirsty and sick and imprisoned. Such giving is an act of true worship. There is a close connection between how we treat each other and how we treat God. In Matthew's gospel, Jesus says that whatever we do for one of the least of his brothers and sisters, we do for him.[6] God takes these acts of love (or moments of rejection) very personally.

And why wouldn't he? Jesus himself was poor. He chose to be born into the poverty of a family struggling beneath the heel of Imperial Rome. Writer Scott Bessenecker suggests that "the very first statement Jesus ever voiced about his concern for the poor, oppressed, marginalized people was when he cried out as one of them—eyes shut tight, mouth open wide, wailing, kicking.... It was one of the most profound acts of solidarity with the poor he could make."[7] For all of the other aspects of his Advent we celebrate each year, let us not forget this part of the story: "When God voted with his birth, he voted for the poor."[8]

OUR TURN

We cannot allow the broken and vulnerable to become invisible. Which brings us back to how Christmas can still change the world. Let's return to Jesus' words in Matthew 25:

> *You shall be richly rewarded,* for when I was hungry, you fed Me. And when I was thirsty, you gave Me something to drink. I was alone as a stranger, and you welcomed Me *into your homes and into your lives.* I was naked, and you gave Me clothes to wear; I was sick, and you tended to My needs; I was in prison, and you comforted Me.[9]

These are very simple acts of service being described—giving someone something to eat or drink, welcoming them, clothing them, visiting them. Simple as they are, these gifts matter very much to Jesus—and to those in need. So why not start there? Sometimes we will be led to huge, global strategies (more on that in the next chapter), but it's usually the simple, common-sense acts of love that make the difference.

Think of a single parent "adopted" anonymously by someone at church, provided with toys for the kids, groceries, gas cards—that's the world being changed. Think of a family that decides to serve in a local shelter—the poor are cared for and the family members' hearts become a bit more like God's.

Picture entire churches deciding that some of the money they are saving by giving relationally and resisting cultural norms should be given to the "least of these" in our communities and world—that's when Christmas still makes a difference. Businesses find ways to get involved. Students get creative about giving to other kids they may never meet. The presents around the tree aren't stacked quite so high, but the stories of worship and love grow richer and deeper. Children start telling their parents they want less for Christmas so that others might have more. People of all ages are finding themselves with generous hearts, offering their time, money, and selves to others because they are compelled by the love of God.

Through this kind of radical but practical giving, we are transformed by the Advent story. But make no mistake: the changes that occur are not simply about us. God is up to something in his world. When God's people serve the poor in humble, generous ways, the story of Jesus is told again and again. The poor in our world will be touched by God through how we choose to celebrate Christmas.

Of course, as Reggie McNeal reminds us, "God is the One doing the heavy lifting!"[10] Through his trustworthy Spirit, God is sending us into a broken but beautiful world on which he will never give up. When we show up and love in the name of God, God shows up. That's part of the mystery of partnering with Jesus in the work he is still doing.

> A woman gave her German-speaking dad a "Save the Date" card for a surprise night out. Since he has Parkinson's and doesn't go out much, the woman's dad enjoyed the German choir concert more than she could have realized.

In this decidedly cynical world, where far too many people have heard far too many empty words, the way we love others makes a difference—whether the others live in the third world or the third house down the street.

A BEAUTIFUL BODY

We believe that each of these beautiful acts of love will combine together to form a movement that changes the world. The Advent Conspiracy isn't simply about individuals or single churches giving people a sense of who Jesus is—it's about the entire Body of Christ at work in the world. As we worship fully, spend less, give more, and love all, something begins to form that is greater than any single person or denomination. We celebrate other ministries. We focus on places in our own communities and around the world where we can combine our efforts with our brothers and sisters. As we love our neighbors *and* one another, the Kingdom of God grows and the world takes notice.[11]

This is why we suggest that each organization—from churches to student ministries to parachurch groups—gather an offering of the money saved by giving relationally and resisting consumerism. We want to be clear: we don't want your money. Not a dime of what any organization collects will be given to this thing we call the Advent Conspiracy. Instead, we ask that each organization take whatever money it raises and prayerfully give it to those who need it most.

We also ask participants to consider what it would mean to partner with others of like heart and mind. It is amazing to see how much good can be done in the world when we join others. In 2006, only five churches participated in this Conspiracy and they collected nearly half a million dollars! Imagine what would happen if thousands of churches joined together in telling the world about Jesus' birth *and* in living out the story of his sacrificial love.

The poor and vulnerable and outcast will be seen and heard and touched and fed—not out of some class-based guilt, but as an act of worship. We must not

"Because of Advent Conspiracy and Living Water, my parents told us that they had looked forward to Christmas more this year than any other year. The real value of Advent Conspiracy for my family was that we were able to articulate desires already deep in our souls."

forget that. The good news of the gospel is for all people, including us. We are all poor and blind and imprisoned. We are the ones who have been given this lavish gift of life with God, and now we are called to enter this broken world and love differently. When we do, Christmas can still change the world.

A few months after Christmas we received word from Living Water International that the funds we had collected in December were now being used to dig wells in Liberia. It was happening because children on the other side of the world saved their pennies, families celebrated Christmas differently, students creatively pooled their resources, and churches took offerings. People in western Africa who these folks would never meet this side of heaven were about to be loved in a practical and biblical way. Cup after cup of clean water would be given in the name of Jesus. Who knows where the conversations might lead?

The first well was dug for a village that used to drink from a swamp, and for a chief who had given up on the name of Jesus.

[7]

WHAT IF?

What if Advent is bigger than we dare imagine?

The story of God's Son entering our world is the point of our worship and celebration each Christmas. Because of his great love, God moved into the neighborhood and we now have hope. But the Incarnation is not something to be celebrated only once a year. The story is bigger than that—and it's still being written.

The clear teaching of Scripture shows that we are being sent into this broken world to both *tell* the great story of God's love and to *live* it. Our lives are to give others a picture of our Savior. As the apostle Paul reminds us, we are "representatives of the Liberating King."[1]

By trusting in his Spirit who lives in us, we can be to a hurting world God's presence and beauty and glory and power in bigger ways than we ever thought possible.

God is *still* moving into the neighborhood! The Incarnation isn't about only the *one* glorious moment in history when Jesus walked this earth—it's also about a God who still wants to make an appearance in this world through his followers.

Can we even begin to imagine what would happen if the followers of Jesus around the world started to live this truth? What would happen if we decided not simply to celebrate the Advent of Christ, but to combat the leading cause of death in a practical way?

What if, together, we did something about the water crisis?

We don't have to walk but a few feet to spin a knob and have clean water for drinking, bathing, watering the lawn and garden (and kids, if yours are anything

[A church collected just over $12,000 in their Christmas offering. They split the funds three ways for three charities—one local, one national, and one global. The donation to the national charity received a matching grant, so the $4,000 gift became $8,000.]

like ours), washing the dog and car and boat . . . it is shocking to think about how much of our water we watch simply run off.

In Liberia we met people who were collecting drinking water from the same cesspool that killed family members the week before. We met women and children who walked for miles to fill and carry twenty liters or more of water each day. Stagnant, disease-infested pond water. Sludge. Mud. Sewage runoff water. According to the World Water Council:

- 1.1 billion people lack access to safe drinking water,
- 2.6 billion people lack adequate sanitation,
- 1.8 million people die every year from diarrheal diseases, 90 percent of whom are children under [the age of] five,
- 3,900 children die every day because of dirty water or poor hygiene.[2]

Let's confront that reality again: nearly four thousand children die every day . . . from dirty water. That is roughly 1.4 million children who die each year. As we saw in the previous chapter, each statistic is always someone's daughter, someone's son. If they aren't dying, they are trudging to cesspools or polluted public taps for water. Can you imagine the time spent walking, waiting, pumping, and returning home with twenty liters of water on your back? Being relieved of the burden of collecting and drinking unclean water gives youths (young girls especially) the ability to learn skills in school that will help them escape poverty. It reduces the amount of infant and toddler deaths, increases the productivity of adults, and extends the lives of the elderly.[3]

Clean water for every person in the world. This is our dream, and, yes, it's a big one.

EXCHANGING CONSUMPTION FOR COMPASSION

Together, we are greater than we are apart. The Advent of Christ is an opportunity to declare to the world that God has given us the greatest gift. Advent Conspiracy exists to help the church awaken, realign with God's movement, and worship Jesus wholly at Christmas—and thus be transformed by the God of Advent.

What if, in the coming years, Christ-followers around the world started a countercultural movement that reached far beyond a few days each December? What if we resisted the empire of "more" even as our worship echoed throughout the year? What if the story of God drawing near compelled us to love those living on the margins of our world? What if we joined together—across lines that often separate us—to serve both local communities and remote villages in the name of Jesus? Perhaps we could reclaim the story of Christmas, and the world would once again take notice.

To those entering the Conspiracy, we ask you now to bring this dream to a reality. Consider new collaborations with others in your community as together you serve those in your midst. Imagine what might happen if people in your group or church partnered with others across the city who are longing to celebrate this Christmas differently. How might the world be different this next year? How might *you* be different?

What would happen if together, acting as one body, the followers of Jesus joined together to address the global water crisis? We are inviting our co-conspirators to designate at least 25 percent of their Christmas gift offering to clean water projects around the globe. Is it possible that this leading cause of death and disease might fade into an afterthought someday? Imagine the dramatic impression such a movement would have on the world's opinion of those who love and serve the one true God. As we strive toward equality in the basic necessities of life, let us never forget that Jesus is the Water of Life. He values life . . . are you ready to place that value above all else at Christmas time?

What if Christmas was no longer about *stuff*? What if, this Christmas, we could spend less, give more, worship fully, and love all? What if we did that all year long?

Then we would raise our glasses high, filled to overflowing with the Living Water that is Jesus, and worship our God who covers all need. Our lives and houses would be full—not of stuff, but of substance, of divine presence, of life!

What if we vowed to do this together? What if God's conspiracy began to transform people from every tribe, tongue, and nation? This is our invitation. This is our prayer.

To the glory of our God—Loving Father, Incarnate Son, Holy Spirit—Christmas can still change the world.

LETTERS FROM CO-CONSPIRATORS

Just a few weeks before Christmas our pastor announced that we would be taking an offering for clean drinking water at our Christmas Eve service. Pretty amazing! My husband and I are so blessed. . . . This all started in January of '08 when we caught up on podcasts from Imago Dei on our way home from the holidays with family.

I just wanted to let you know we received $44,000 for water wells that night . . . hooray!

Lynn
Austin, Texas

Dear AC: Thanks for all the great resources for the Advent Conspiracy. We had a wonderful Advent because of it. We set a goal to raise $18,000 and ended up receiving $72,000! We sent it to the water fund to drill eight wells in rural Zambia.

Mark
Cincinnati, Ohio

We should probably raise around $1,500 for wells in Haiti. We are going to repair a well in a village we already work with and give the rest to [the] Haiti Water Project. A group of women in church along with a few artists created ornaments in the shape of water drops to help the people make the connection. We also moved the water table in the church across the room and made it "inconvenient" for people to get water while at Mosaic [Church] to illustrate the point.... People thought that was cool.

We printed our own Christmas cards to have the Mosaic peeps hand out to their friends, with plenty of space to write a personal note ... to encourage relational giving.... Thanks for the inspiration and the provoking unto good works.... This is our second year conspiring to overthrow the empire of greed.... This was the best yet.

Kevin
Miami, Florida

I just wanted to let you know how our Advent Conspiracy movement affected our church and community this Christmas season.... We focused on the four parts of Advent with different suggestions for people to get involved.... [One week we had a] "give more" day [where] we challenged the church to not come to our church building for a service that morning as usual—but to go out into the community and be the church! It was fantastic to hear stories of people inviting their neighbors over for a brunch, delivering [baked goods] in their neighborhood, visiting nursing homes, serving in a soup kitchen, having family church at home.... It was a great way for us to spend time with others who we wouldn't go to church with. For spend[ing] less, we raised money for water projects, which we gave to two organizations we are involved with as a church—$30,000 was raised, and we know some just gave directly to the project of their choice. Praise God for all that clean water that was shared with others!

Maryanne
Saskatoon, Saskatchewan, Canada

... Besides asking people to spend half as much on gifts, we also had a water week and a rice week. During water week people drank water only and set aside the money they would have spent on other drinks to donate to Living Water. We did a similar thing the next week, but challenged families to eat only rice for three dinners and put aside the money they would have spent on groceries or eating out. I think all of these things really drove home the message of how blessed we are. As I spoke through the four themes of Advent Conspiracy in my sermons, I was struck by a thought as I was writing my message one day. It struck me that because of our participation and "sacrifices," children that were going to die in 2009 from waterborne illnesses were going to live and get healthy, and parents who were going to mourn the loss of their children would not have to endure that awful fate. They instead would celebrate the presence of clean water in their community and would hopefully wonder what motivated people in America to provide it for them, and would find that the answer was Jesus.

We are a church of 175 . . . and collected over $13,000 this year toward the Advent Conspiracy.

Bob
St. Joseph, Missouri

Dear AC: Our family chose not to exchange gifts for adults this year. Instead we signed up to serve a meal on Christmas Eve day at a rescue mission. We took the grandchildren along and they served bottles of water while we dished up the meal.

I was satisfied that although the task we did was nothing big, we made a conscious choice to give instead of receive. Hopefully it pleased the Lord and sent a message to the young ones about the way Christ wants us to live each and every day.

Jan
Vancouver, Washington

This is my first year in a parish, and I ran across the Advent Conspiracy website with very little time to prepare. The leadership pulled together, however, and we were able to present the call to live a more simple Christmas season all four Advent Sundays. On Christmas Day we held a single offering to be given to the Christian Reformed World Relief Committee to purchase wells for communities that do not have access to clean drinking water ($250 buys one well). Our church of 220 active members raised just over $50,000. God is good.

Chad
Charlottetown, Prince Edward Island, Canada

Our community has had an awakening in the past year to the poverty next door. Homeless relief and homeless prevention has moved to the forefront of church priorities and the Advent Conspiracy gave us an opportunity to make a significant statement over the holidays. We did a talk on transformation and showed the AC promo to illuminate that it often starts with the day-to-day shift in awareness of how you and others around you are living. So, we wrapped up a huge cardboard box as a giant present, with a slot on the top, and asked the people ... over the next four weeks [to] consider giving up one gift and putting those funds in the box, with the money going toward homeless relief/prevention. We counted the money and wrapped the number in a smaller box that we opened on Christmas Eve; $21,000 was raised. We were able to present the check the following Sunday to the designated agencies as well as have our mayor and county supervisor come out and share their gratitude to us as a faith community leading the way in caring for our city.

Jesse
Ventura, California

Coming off a November in which the congregation stepped up to the plate in a *huge* way both financially and with their time to help with a Thanksgiving project we put together, we decided that it would be best to set "modestly aggressive" goals for our Advent Conspiracy campaign. First, we decided to participate in a local coat drive to help provide underprivileged kids with winter coats. We felt 200 coats was a realistic goal. Second, we decided to see if we could raise

$5,000 to drill one clean water well through Living Water International.

Each week the coats kept rolling in, until we had finally pulled together 275 winter coats by the end of the month. We were just blown away by that. But what was more surprising was the way in which people gave for Living Water International. The first week, over $6,000 came in, surpassing our monthly goal in *one week*! We were suspicious at that point that we had hit our high point for the month, and that giving would drop dramatically the next week and slowly taper off throughout the month. We were *so* wrong. . . . When it was all said and done, we pulled together nearly $27,500, which we'll be using to drill five clean water wells in Guatemala through Living Water International. The Advent Conspiracy impacted our congregation in a way that will not soon be forgotten, inspiring us to pursue a "get your hands dirty" kind of Christmas spirituality that worships Jesus as it remembers the poor. Thanks for letting us be a part of the story.

Andrew
Tulsa, Oklahoma

ACKNOWLEDGMENTS

Rick, Chris, and Greg would like to acknowledge some of the people who have made not only this book, but this movement, a reality. A special thanks goes to:

Our three wives, who have supported our Kingdom dreams along the way.

Jeanne McKinley, for directing and guiding this Conspiracy as it grew from a handful of churches to a global movement.

The fellow pastors and staff in our three churches — it's a privilege to serve alongside you.

Clint Kemp and Ted Baird, for your vision and for being there at the very beginning.

Ken Weigel, for gracefully steering three busy pastors and keeping us on a miraculous timeline.

Tony Biaggne, for sharing his mind-stretching creativity at every level of this Conspiracy.

Jon Collins and Brian Hall, for putting the vision of Advent Conspiracy within one of the best short videos we've ever seen.

Mike Foster and Plain Joe Studios, for giving us their time, talent, and the logo that got Advent Conspiracy started.

Scott Andreas with design + technology for do-gooders, for his huge personal heart for Advent Conspiracy and the incredible website that started telling the AC story in 2007.

Kelly Hall, for taking the words of three different voices and making them somehow sound as one.

Angela Scheff and the team at Zondervan.

Chris Ferebee, for making this book happen.

Stan Patyrak and the folks at Living Water International. It's an honor to partner with you as you give a cup of clean water in Jesus' name.

The people of Imago Dei, Ecclesia, and The Crossing. Your generosity and passion for people you may never meet astounds and inspires us. Oh, how God is smiling.

Our co-conspirators around the world. Together we now live out the story of Jesus, our Savior come to earth. Yes, Christmas can still change the world.

SMALL GROUP DVD DISCUSSION GUIDE

HOW TO USE THE DISCUSSION GUIDE

This discussion guide was developed for use with the *Advent Conspiracy* four-session DVD, which complements and further develops the material in this book. Ideally, those leading a group discussion on *Advent Conspiracy* should preview each DVD session and read through the accompanying portion of the discussion guide beforehand. While the material in this discussion guide is intended for use with the DVD, many of the discussion questions can also be used for discussion of the book.

The sessions cover the four main ideas of *Advent Conspiracy* and can be matched with the following chapters in the book:

Session	**Book Chapter(s)**
1. Worship Fully	1 and 3
2. Spend Less	2 and 4
3. Give More	5
4. Love All	6 and 7

The following format is suggested when using the discussion guide, but feel free to adapt the material to fit your own context.

OPENING QUESTIONS

These are open-ended questions and ice-breakers that you can use to begin the discussion.

DVD VIEWING

The DVD clip for each session is approximately 15 minutes long.

DVD DISCUSSION

These are questions that follow up the video teaching and engage the group in discussion of the content they just watched.

ENGAGING THE WORD

These are portions of Scripture for group study and discussion that tie in with the theme of the session.

UNWRAPPING THE MESSAGE

This section contains some final thoughts, questions, and ways of applying the teaching material.

[SESSION 1]

WORSHIP FULLY

OPENING QUESTIONS

1. Most of us have very specific memories about the Christmas season, both positive and negative. What are some of those positive memories? How would you describe the best Christmas you ever had as a child? What made it special for you?

2. Do you still look forward to the Christmas season? If so, what do you enjoy about the season? If you no longer look forward to Christmas, why not?

3. What word would best describe what you want to experience this year during the Christmas season? What are some obstacles that get in the way of that happening?

DVD VIEWING

Watch the video clip for Session 1.

DVD DISCUSSION

1. When the authors suggest that the Advent Conspiracy is an invitation to "remain in the gospel of Jesus," what do you think they mean? What does that mean for you?

2. What practical choices do you need to make to ensure that the Christmas season remains a time of focused worship? How might you remind and encourage each other as friends to do this? As a family? As a church?

ENGAGING THE WORD

Read Luke 2:8–20 together as a group.

1. The shepherds are well-known participants in the Christmas narrative. Think about images you have seen on traditional Christmas cards, nativity scenes, or even the way shepherds are portrayed in a typical church Christmas program. How have we been led to picture these first visitors to the manger?

In this passage, we are told that the shepherds were a socially despised group (poor, criminal, outcast). Can you think of any parallels to this group today?

The shepherds are the first ones to whom the angels announced the birth of Christ. What does that tell us about the heart of God toward social outcasts? How does this relate to the message of Christmas?

2. In what ways does the worship of the shepherds differ from our celebration of Christmas? What are some specific ways in which our contemporary celebration of Christmas moves us away from the worship the shepherds experienced? What can we do to recapture that sense of wonder and gratitude?

UNWRAPPING THE MESSAGE

1. We see the shepherds not only approaching the manger in a spirit of worship, we see them moving into their world to proclaim the good news. The announcement that God has given us his Son changes everything. Who still needs to hear this good news?

   Think of some specific people and ways that your family, group, or church can bring this announcement to the world? What might that look like this Christmas?

2. God has drawn near. He was born as a baby that night in Bethlehem. Through Jesus, he walked among us and the story forever changed. This is what we celebrate each Christmas. This is what the songs proclaim. This is the story we tell to the world each year. What if the choices that we make this year about our spending and the way we give gifts to one another were a part of our worship?

   The Advent season is our chance to celebrate the wondrous moment when God entered our world to make things right. It is a season of worship. This is the foundation for our conspiracy. Close this session by praying as a group for a fresh encounter with God during this season of Advent. Pray for a desire to worship more fully and for opportunities to enter into the ongoing story of Jesus and his work in this world.

> "Understand what you're doing and why you're doing it. This is not about anger, disgust, or guilt—it is about entering the story of Jesus more deeply with a desire to worship more fully. It is not enough to say no to the way Christmas is celebrated by many; we need to say yes to a different way of celebrating."
>
> **From Chapter 1,** *Advent Conspiracy*

Optional Reading: Chapters 1 and 3 of *Advent Conspiracy*

[SESSION 2]

SPEND LESS

OPENING QUESTIONS

1. "What do you want for Christmas?" This is a question that many of us have been asked since we were children. But often we don't get what we want. Share with one another about a time (Christmas or otherwise) when you didn't get what you wanted. How did you respond to the disappointment?

2. Now talk about a time when you got *exactly* what you wanted. How long were you satisfied with the gift? How long did the joy last? What can we learn from these experiences?

DVD VIEWING

Watch the video clip for Session 2.

DVD DISCUSSION

1. The authors suggest that the fastest growing religion in the world isn't Islam or Christianity, but "radical consumerism." Do you agree or disagree with this statement? In what ways are we drawn to this kind of worship?

2. Consider all of the advertisements you are exposed to every Christmas. What are some specific examples that have affected you? What emotions do they arouse in you? How might they contribute to a sense that you are lacking something in your life? How can we become more aware and less susceptible to such messages?

ENGAGING THE WORD

Read James 5:1–6 together as a group.

1. What are some of the specific sins that James condemns in this passage? What are some of the consequences that will come to those who put their trust in wealth and riches?

In what ways have you experienced the truth of this passage in your own life? Have you ever purchased something, only to discard it soon after because it had lost its luster? Share an example with the group.

Read Matthew 6:19–24 together as a group.

2. In verses 19 and 20, Jesus draws a comparison between earthly and heavenly treasures. What are the differences between the two types of treasure?

   What do you think Jesus means by verse 21? In what way is our spending during the Christmas season a reflection of our heart? How can you encourage one another this Christmas season to stay focused on the worship of God alone?

UNWRAPPING THE MESSAGE

1. In Chapter 4 of this book, the authors note that "Christmas is a season of excess." Unfortunately, this is more accurate than most of us want to admit. In what way does this season become a "season of excess" for you? Food? Drink? An overstuffed schedule? Overspending? How does this leave you feeling after the holiday is over?

2. As parents, teachers, and adult role models, what does your approach to gift-giving at Christmas teach children about worship? What does it teach them about contentment?

What are some practical ways that you can use this season as an opportunity to teach children how to handle money responsibly? What are the important lessons that you would like to teach them?

Perhaps you come to the end of this session feeling a sense of frustration or even defeat. The struggle against wanting more and more is very real indeed. The unrealistic expectations we place on things that rust and fall apart is a truth that each of us must face.

> "The only sure remedy is a change of heart, and the best place to begin is at the feet of the newborn Jesus."
>
> **From Chapter 4 of** *Advent Conspiracy*

This is the heart of the Advent Conspiracy. More than just an invitation to say no to overspending and mindless gifts, we're asking you to say yes to a new way of celebrating Christmas. When we resist the empire of consumerism, our time and money are freed up and we are able to give relational gifts to others.

Optional Reading: Chapters 2 and 4 of *Advent Conspiracy*

[SESSION 3]

GIVE MORE

OPENING QUESTIONS

1. Everyone makes jokes about the infamous fruitcake, that sweater you'd never wear in public, or any number of other gifts that didn't really have *you* in mind when they were given. Without naming names or getting in trouble with anyone in your group, what's the most impersonal gift you've been given?

2. Now let's be even more honest: what's the most impersonal gift you've ever given? Is there a story behind it you can share?

DVD VIEWING

Watch the video clip for Session 3.

DVD DISCUSSION

1. Most of us have struggled at one point with how best to celebrate Christmas. For some Christians, things have gotten so out of hand that they no longer give gifts to anyone. What are some of the ways that you have chosen to celebrate Christmas?

   What are some of the dangers when we associate love solely with the giving of material objects? What are some other ways that we can give that clearly communicate love?

2. Does the story of St. Nicholas still have meaning for us today? Were you familiar with this story as a child? How might you use this story to bring the gift-giving tradition back to the story of Jesus?

ENGAGING THE WORD

Read John 1:1 – 14 with fresh eyes and fresh ears.

1. How does this passage bring us back to the miracle of Christmas? Share with one another an aspect of the Incarnation that you don't want to forget this Advent.

Read Matthew 1:18–23 and Isaiah 7:14.

2. Discuss the significance of the name "Immanuel." What are some ways that you hope to experience God as "Immanuel" in your own life this Christmas? How can you give the gift of God's presence to others? Think of some specific ideas for giving relationally.

UNWRAPPING THE MESSAGE

1. As you consider what it means to give relationally, what is it that most excites you? What part of this kind of giving will be the biggest challenge for you? What's the biggest risk?

2. Visit the "Rethinking Christmas" website (*www.rethinkingchristmas.com*). Are there any ideas that seemed to fit you? Did reading about other approaches to gift-giving stir up any thoughts for the gifts you'll give this year? Is there a way for your group or church to encourage one another with such an approach?

God was here in flesh and blood and by his life, death, and resurrection, we now have hope. This is what the Incarnation means to us. All the prophecies, all the promises, came down to this one very relational gift. The Father gave the most personal gift ever—his Son.

Now we can creatively give to one another the gift of ourselves. It becomes more about "presence" than "presents." And it is in these moments that others begin to get a sense of who God is. Perhaps even a watching world will take notice as we worship him and love one another. Perhaps as we now take this Conspiracy outside the walls of our own churches and homes, the world itself will be loved and served.

Even as you consider the personal aspects of what it will mean to express love to those who are close to you, remember that God is calling us to love the world outside our current relationships. If the Incarnation is at the heart of the Christmas story, it is still at the heart of our story. In other words, God still wants to move into the neighborhood … every neighborhood. Be sure to read Chapter 6 of this book before your group gathers next.

As you go into the next few days considering the invitation to enter the story with us, listen to the words of William Wilberforce, a follower of Jesus who was instrumental in ending the slave trade in England. Listen to his strong words that call us to do more than talk about doing things differently:

> Get going. Be useful, generous, moderate and self-denying in your manner of life. Treat the lack of positive action on your part as sin. If God chooses to bless you with material prosperity, don't use it on the absurd task of keeping up with the current trends and fads. By using your money modestly and without display, show that you are not a slave to fashion. Be an example of someone who uses his or her wealth for purposes that are more important than showing off or making a big impression. Demonstrate through the way you live that worldly things are not even close to the value of heavenly things.[1]

Optional Reading: Chapter 5 of *Advent Conspiracy*

[SESSION 4]

LOVE ALL

OPENING QUESTION

We've all heard the rally cry to make a difference in this world, but do we really believe that it can happen? When you hear people talk about addressing global issues like poverty, disease, and hunger, what's your reaction? Are you overwhelmed? Skeptical? Excited? Apathetic?

DVD VIEWING

Watch the video clip for Session 4.

DVD DISCUSSION

1. What is your reaction to the story of the village chief and his response to "good news"? Have you ever met anyone with a similar response?

2. When you hear the latest statistic or book that tells you how the world views Christians, what is your honest reaction? Do you get defensive? Angry? Are you indifferent?

ENGAGING THE WORD

Read Luke 2:1–24.

1. Perhaps you and your friends or family have often read Luke 2:1–24 as a Christmas tradition. But consider the dirty manger, the seemingly indifferent community of Bethlehem, the not-too-impressive first visitors after Jesus' birth, and the temple sacrifice of two doves or pigeons (a provision made in Leviticus 12:8 if a lamb was too expensive) . . . all of these are subtle clues that Jesus was born into poverty. Imagine reading this passage through the eyes of someone lacking the same resources as you. How might reading it this way change the way we worship this Christmas?

Read Luke 4:16–21.

2. In what sense are each one of us "the poor" to whom Jesus brings his good news? In addition to this deep spiritual truth, what are some of the practical ways that we can understand Jesus' words?

Read Matthew 25:34–40.

3. In Chapter 5 of this book, the authors suggest: "This Christmas, one of the things that could distinguish a Christ-follower is a love that reaches out to the hungry and thirsty and sick and imprisoned, the unclothed and completely forgotten. What an act of worship this would be. What a glorious gift to those in need, but somehow such love is a gift to Jesus himself."

   In what sense are our acts of mercy and kindness a gift to Jesus? Do you believe that he takes such actions (or lack of them) personally? Does this motivate you to reach out to others? Why or why not?

UNWRAPPING THE MESSAGE

1. If your church or small group were to "love all" this Advent season, what would that look like?

   Is there something your family or friends could do together to love those who might be considered "the least of these"?

2. How do you respond when you hear stories of churches partnering with other churches? How does this type of partnership express unity in the body of Christ?

What are some ways that churches in your community could partner together?

Can Christmas still change the world? Hopefully by now you're realizing that we believe the Advent of our Savior is the moment on which all our hopes rest. We believe that first Christmas really did *forever* change the world. But we are asking you to consider the possibility that the *way* we celebrate the birth of Jesus can *also* change the world. Like never before, our world is in dire need of good news. And we can share the very good news of God coming to earth. We can tell that story in both word and deed. The hope, the restoration, the forgiveness, the compassion, and the sheer generosity of God—this is what people need to see and know and trust. As we laugh and celebrate and mourn and grieve and serve and notice and touch the lives of others, we reflect the very love of God. And we believe that when we love as we have been so outrageously loved, Christmas can still bring change to the world.

Optional Reading: Chapters 6 and 7 of *Advent Conspiracy*

NOTES

CHAPTER 2: THE RELIGION OF CONSUMERISM

1. For an excellent treatment of this issue, see William T. Cavanaugh's book, *Being Consumed* (Grand Rapids, Mich.: W. B. Eerdmans, 2008).
2. James 5:2–6.
3. Luke 12:15.
4. See Numbers 11:18–20.
5. Ralph Winter, "Reconsecration to a Wartime, Not a Peacetime, Lifestyle," *Perspectives on the World Christian Movement* (Pasadena, Calif.: William Carey Library, 1981), 814.

CHAPTER 3: WORSHIP FULLY

1. Luke 1:38.
2. Luke 1:46–55 NIV.
3. Mark Labberton, *The Dangerous Act of Worship* (Downers Grove, Ill.: InterVarsity, 2007), 37–38.
4. Matthew 1:23 NIV (see Isaiah 7:14).

CHAPTER 4: SPEND LESS

1. Matthew 6:24.
2. 2 Corinthians 8:13–14.
3. 1 Timothy 6:10.
4. 1 Timothy 6:9.
5. 2 Corinthians 9:11.
6. C. S. Lewis, *Mere Christianity* (New York: HarperCollins, 2001), 86.

CHAPTER 5: GIVE MORE

1. John 1:1–3 NIV.
2. John 1:1–3.
3. John 1:14 NIV.
4. Alan Hirsch, *The Forgotten Ways: Reactivating the Missional Church* (Grand Rapids, Mich.: Brazos, 2006), 131.
5. John 10:30.
6. John 14:9.
7. N. T. Wright, *Simply Christian: Why Christianity Makes Sense* (San Francisco: HarperSanFrancisco, 2006), 140.

8. On the Advent Conspiracy website (*www.adventconspiracy.org*), you'll find a section entitled "Rethinking Christmas." This is a resource intended to encourage discussions and idea-sharing when it comes to what we're now referring to as relational gifts. This might be a great place for some of you to start. Read what others are trying and then make it your own. Share a completely new idea that's occurred to no one else. What the three of us have discovered at each of our churches is that once you begin thinking differently and learn what others have tried, you start coming up with your own amazing ideas that connect back to this beautiful story of Christmas.

9. Alan Hirsch in his book *The Forgotten Ways* (p. 131) identifies various dimensions that help us understand the "Incarnation of God in Jesus the Messiah." Though we won't fully discuss them here (or in some cases, even use the same terms), we want to acknowledge his and Michael Frost's contribution to our thinking.

10. Matthew 1:23 NIV (see Isaiah 7:14).

11. See Colossians 1:15.

12. Luke 2:11.

13. See Philippians 2:6.

14. Alan Hirsch, *The Forgotten Ways,* 134.

15. Mark 10:45.

CHAPTER 6: LOVE ALL

1. Jeremiah 2:13.
2. Scot McKnight, *Embracing Grace: A Gospel for All of Us* (Brewster, Mass.: Paraclete, 2005), 80–81.
3. Luke 4:18.
4. Luke 4.
5. 2 Corinthians 8:9.
6. Matthew 25:40.
7. Scott A. Bessenecker, *The New Friars: The Emerging Movement Serving the World's Poor* (Downers Grove, Ill.: InterVarsity, 2006), 59–60.
8. Ibid.
9. Matthew 25:35–36.
10. Reggie McNeal, *Missional Renaissance* (San Francisco: Jossey-Bass, 2009), 35.
11. John 17:20–23.

CHAPTER 7: WHAT IF?

1. 2 Corinthians 5:20.
2. World Water Council, *www.worldwatercouncil.org/index .php?id=23.*
3. Ibid.

SESSION 3: GIVE MORE

1. Bob Beltz, *Real Christianity: A Paraphrase in Modern English of "A Practical View of the Prevailing Religious System of Professed Christians in the Higher and Middle Classes in This Country, Contrasted with Real Christianity,"* published in 1797 by William Wilberforce, Esq. Member of Parliament for the County of York. (Ventura, Calif.: Regal Books, 2006), 23.

Advent Conspiracy DVD

Can Christmas Still Change the World?

Rick McKinley, Chris Seay, and Greg Holder

Are you fed up with how consumerism has stolen the soul of Christmas? This year, take a stand! Join the growing groundswell of Christ-followers who are choosing to making Christmas what it should be—a joyous celebration of Jesus' birth, not a retail circus.

In four compelling sessions, *Advent Conspiracy* invites individuals, families, groups, and entire churches to substitute compassion for consumerism by practicing four simple but powerful, countercultural concepts:

Worship Fully—because Christmas begins and ends with Jesus!

Spend Less—and free your resources for things that truly matter.

Give More—of your presence: your hands, your words, your time, your heart.

Love All—the poor, the forgotten, the marginalized, the sick, in ways that make a difference.

Advent Conspiracy DVD session titles:

SESSION 1: Worship Fully
SESSION 2: Spend Less
SESSION 3: Give More
SESSION 4: Love All

Designed for use with *Advent Conspiracy* book, which contains the Small Group DVD Discussion Guide

DVD: 978-0-310-32442-3